For They Shall Be Comforted

For They Shall Be Comforted

By
Alma P. and Clea M. Burton

This book is not an official publication of The Church of Jesus Christ of Latter-day Saints. The opinions and views expressed herein belong solely to the author and do not necessarily represent the opinions or views of Cedar Fort, Inc. Permission for the use of sources, graphics, and photos is also solely the responsibility of the author.

ISBN 13: 978-1-55517-168-1

Published by CFI, an imprint of Cedar Fort, Inc., 2373 W. 700 S., Springville, UT, 84663
Distributed by Cedar Fort, Inc. www.cedarfort.com

Cover design by Lyle Mortimer
Page Layout and Design by Stephen J. Bons

Printed in the United States of America

10 9 8 7 6 5 4

Printed on acid-free paper

DEDICATION

To the Memory of Our Parents—
May Pexton Burton, 1880-1981
Thomas Hyrum Burton, 1878-1930
Ethel Rich Morgan, 1884-1963
John Samuel Morgan, 1882-1963

ACKNOWLEDGMENT

Permission to use certain items in this compilation has been secured either from the individual or the publisher. Grateful acknowledgment is expressed to all whose selections are used in this collection.

We also express our sincere appreciation to our daughter Mrs. Art (Barbara) Barron for her valuable assistance in the initial preparation of this book.

FOREWORD

When sorrow or grief comes to us or our loved ones, our souls reach out for comfort and assistance. At such times we seek meaningful explanations of life and its purposes.

Messages of inspiration, hope, and comfort have been given by many people—those of past generations as well as those of today. A few of these expressions have been collected and compiled in this small volume.

The compilers of this book sincerely hope that those who read its pages will be filled with added faith and trust in an ever-loving Father and will gain a clearer understanding of the purposes of life, death, and the resurrection—that they may be comforted.

TABLE OF CONTENTS

CHAPTER ONE
Why?

*W*ho in time of sorrow or grief has not asked the question, Why? Why did this happen to me? Why must I suffer disappointment and experience such sadness? Or, Why did my loved one die?

Trials come to us for our instruction and blessing. The Lord knows our heartaches, our anguish and our grief. He could give the answer to our question, Why? but he refrains, knowing that our faith in him and in his purposes will increase through our prayerful searching. He has given us the assurance that death is not the end, that this mortal existence is but one part of the great plan of the Master Architect.

The Lord will not leave us comfortless. He is our Father and our God and is interested in each of us. He will hear our earnest petitions and in his own time will give the answer to our question, Why?

*W*e know, that the issue of life and death and the welfare of the human family are in the hands of our Great Creator; The wisdom of the Almighty we begin to comprehend to such a degree that we feel to leave all things in his hands after we have done our whole duty, after we have prayed and fasted and worked for the restoration of the sick. We feel that the Father is over all, and that by his power are the sick raised from their beds of affliction; and without his good pleasure we cannot realize the blessings that we in our finite wisdom think we ought to possess. It is proper that our Heavenly Father should hold within his grasp the welfare of his children in life and death.

—Seymour B. Young

The ever-present expectancy of death is never far removed from any of us—whether we realize it or not. None of us can avoid it. It comes alike to the great and to the unknown; to the righteous and to the unrighteous. Wherein we differ is not in our ability to avert it, but in the preparedness with which we meet it. At such times some question the judgments of God. Some find bitterness because of the circumstances and because of the seeming untimeliness of death. With our limited understanding, often we do not agree with the time and the place and the manner in which men come and go. We see many live and prosper, who, according to our way of thinking may not deserve to do either. We see many die, who, in our judgment, have earned the right to live and whose presence among us is sorely needed. And if, with our limited perspective and understanding, we were called upon to give an explanation of the pattern of life and death as it daily takes shape before our eyes, we might be led to conclude that in it all there is lack of purpose, lack of justice, lack of consistency. But fortunately for us and for all men, it has not been given unto us to judge, nor to execute, nor to measure out the days and the years of men. We may be most grateful that such matters belong to the Lord God our Father, who sees things past and things to come. And, we may be grateful for the assurance that there is plan and purpose in this world, and in our own lives.

—Richard L. Evans

When we get into the spirit world, and the veil is withdrawn, we shall then perhaps understand the whys and wherefores.

—Wilford Woodruff

Should we be protected always from hardship, pain, suffering, sacrifice or labor? Should the Lord protect the righteous? Should He immediately punish the wicked? If growth comes from fun and ease and aimless irresponsibility, then why should we ever exert ourselves to work or learn or overcome? If success is measured by the years we live, then early death is failure and tragedy. If earth life is the ultimate, how can we justify death ever, even in old age? If we look at mortality as a complete existence, then pain, sorrow, failure, and short life could be a calamity. But if we look upon the whole life as an eternal thing stretching far into the pre-mortal past and into the eternal postdeath future, then all happenings may be in proper perspective and may fall into proper place.

—Spencer W. Kimball

What can you know, except by its opposite? Who could number the days, if there were no nights to divide the day from the night? Angels could not enjoy the blessings of light eternal, were there no darkness. All that are exalted and all that will be exalted will be exalted upon this principle. If I do not taste the pangs of death in my mortal body, I never shall know the enjoyment of eternal life. If I do not know pain, I cannot enjoy ease. If I am not acquainted with the dark, the gloomy, the sorrowful, I cannot enjoy the light, the joyous, the felicitous that are ordained for man. No person, either in heaven or upon earth, can enjoy and understand these things upon any other principle.

—Brigham Young

If all the skies were sunshine
   Our faces would be fain
To feel once more upon them
   The cooling splash of rain.
If all the world were music,
   Our hearts would often long
For one sweet strain of silence,
   To break the endless song.
If life were always merry,
   Our souls would seek relief,

And rest from weary laughter
In the quiet arms of grief.
—Henry Van Dyke

Thou art never at any time nearer to God than when under tribulation, which he permits for the purification and beautifying of thy soul.

—Molinos

No pain that we suffer, no trial that we experience is wasted. It ministers to our education, to the development of such qualities as patience, faith, fortitude and humility. All that we suffer and all that we endure, especially when we endure it patiently, builds up our characters, purifies our hearts, expands our souls, and makes us more tender and charitable, more worthy to be called the children of God ... and it is through sorrow and suffering, toil and tribulation, that we gain the education that we come here to acquire and which will make us more like our Father and Mother in heaven.

—Orson F. Whitney

God had one Son on earth without sin, but never one without suffering.

—Augustine

It is necessary we suffer in all things, that we may be qualified and worthy to rule and govern all things. Even as our Father in heaven and his Eldest Son, Jesus.

—Lorenzo Snow

Who ne'er his bread in sorrow ate,
    Who ne'er the mournful midnight hours
Weeping upon his bed has sate,
    He knows you not, ye Heavenly Powers.

—Longfellow

We have been called to pass through trials many times, and I do not think we should complain, because if we had no trials we should hardly feel at home in the other world in the company of the prophets and apostles who were sawn asunder, crucified, etc., for the word of God and testimony of Jesus Christ.

—Wilford Woodruff

All intelligent beings who are crowned with crowns of glory, immortality, and eternal lives must pass through every ordeal appointed for intelligent beings to pass through, to gain their glory and exaltation. Every calamity that can come upon mortal beings will be suffered to come upon the few, to prepare them to enjoy the presence of the Lord. If we obtain the glory that Abraham obtained, we must do so by the same means that he did ... we must pass through the same experience and gain the knowledge, intelligence, and endowments that will prepare us to enter into the celestial kingdom of our Father and God....Every trial and experience you have passed through is necessary for your salvation.

—Brigham Young

It is trial that proves one thing weak and another strong—A house built on the sand is in fair weather just as good as if built on a rock.—A cobweb is as good as the mightiest cable when there is no strain upon it.

—Henry Ward Beecher

I have learned, in whatsoever state I am, therewith to be content.

—Phillippians 4:11

There are few of us but who have been touched somehow by death. Some may not have been touched closely by it nor yet have kept vigil with it, but somewhere along our lives, most of us are sorely bereft of someone near and deeply cherished—and all of us will some day meet it face to face. Perhaps most of us feel that we could accept death for ourselves and for those we love if it did not often seem to come with such untimeliness. But we rebel when it so little considers our wishes or our readiness. But we may well ask ourselves when would we be willing to part with or to part from those we love? And who is there among us whose judgment we would trust to measure out our lives? Such decisions would be terrible for mere men to make. But fortunately we are spared making them;

fortunately they are made by wisdom higher than ours. And when death makes its visitations among us, inconsolable grief and rebellious bitterness should have no place. There must be no quarrel with irrevocable facts. Even when death comes by events which seem unnecessary and avoidable. We must learn to accept what we cannot help. Indeed, the greatest blessing that can follow the death of those we love is reconciliation. Without it there is no peace. But with it come quiet thoughts and quickened memories. And what else shall a man do except become reconciled? What purpose does he serve by fighting what he cannot touch or by brooding upon what he cannot change? We have to trust the Lord God for so many things, and it is but one thing more to trust him in the issues of life and earth, and to accept the fact that his plans and promises and purposes transcend the bounds of this world and of this life. With such faith the years are kind, and peace and reconciliation do come to those who have laid to rest their loved ones—who, even in death, are not far removed from us, and of whom our Father in heaven will be mindful until we meet again, even as we are mindful of our own children. Bitter grief without reconciliation serves no good purpose. Death comes to all of us, but so does life everlasting.

—Richard L. Evans

A Prayer:
O Father, help me understand,
   And know the reason why

The boy that Thou dids't give to me,
   So early had to die;
Why once whose life had been so pure,
   Who never knew deceit,
Should droop and wither like a flower
   Crushed under ruthless feet.

O Father, help me understand
   Thy purposes Divine,
In letting death, with ruthless hand
   Tear his dear heart from mine.
O let me see the veil beyond,
   Where dwells his spirit pure,
And know he's happy where he's gone;
   O let me feel secure.

Forgive the surging doubts that rise
   Within my aching heart,
And take the dimness from mine eyes
   Let darkness all depart.

Let light and knowledge come to me
   From heaven, Thy home on high,
O help me put my trust in Thee:
   O Father, tell me, why.

Perhaps I sin in asking this,
   More faith should show in Thee;
But, O I miss his loving kiss,
   He was so dear to me.
Just let me know that I sometime
   Shall find him, once again,
And clasp again his form to mine:
   I ask, in Jesus' name.
The Answer:
Grieve not, my son for time shall be,

When death shall be no more.
Thy loved one I'll return to thee,
   To cherish evermore..
'Twas in the plan that man should die,
   And slumber in the grave,
But rise again, as even I,
   For this my life I gave.

For mortal life is but a part
   Of God's eternity,
In which the souls of men embark
   To find felicity.
What men call death is but a step
   From low to higher plane,
And all who in the dust have slept,
   Through me shall live again.

Then grieve not for the one that's gone,
   Nor let your heart despair;
For God in wisdom called your son,
   To work for Him up there;
The prison gates to open wide
   For those who died in sin,
And through repentance them to guide
   Again to worship Him.

Let this then be your answer, why,
   And let your heart rejoice,
For unto God they do not die,
   Who answer to His voice;
But walk with Him in realms of love,
   Where all the righteous be.
Be comforted, for there above,
   Thy boy will welcome thee.

—Rey L. Pratt

Anyone can carry his burden, however hard, until nightfall. Anyone can do his work, however hard, for one day. Anyone can live sweetly, patiently, lovingly, purely, till the sun goes down. And this is all that life really means.

—Robert Louis Stevenson

CHAPTER TWO
Spirit Children of God

In time of sorrow and sadness it is comforting to consider and seek to understand the true meaning and full significance of life, and to realize that each phase of life is a part of an eternal plan—God's plan of salvation and exaltation. The Gospel of Jesus Christ provides first for man's existence as a spiritual being prior to birth into mortality, then birth into mortality, followed by death, resurrection, and man's eternal existence as an immortal being.

The Lord revealed to Adam that He created all things spiritually before they were naturally upon the earth. He revealed to Jeremiah that he knew him and that he sanctified and ordained him a Prophet unto the nations before he was born. Paul taught that man has a spirit birth when he wrote to the Hebrews that we have a father of our spirits. And Job declared, "There is a spirit in man, and the inspiration of the Almighty giveth them understanding." It is also written "the dust shall return unto the earth as it was; and the spirit shall return unto God who gave it." The spirit of each of us lived in the presence of God prior to birth into mortality.

Where did we come from? From God. Our spirits existed before they came to this world. They were in the councils of the heavens before the foundations of the earth were laid....We sang together with the heavenly hosts for joy when the foundations of the earth and redemption were mapped out....We were, no doubt, there and took part in all those scenes, we were vitally concerned in the carrying out of these great plans and purposes, we understood them, and it was for our sakes they were decreed and are to be consummated.

         —Joseph F. Smith

At the first organization in heaven we were all present and saw the Savior chosen and appointed and the plan of salvation made, and we sanctioned it.

         —Joseph Smith

Not only was the Savior in the beginning with the Father, but...you and I were there. We dwelt there, and by reason of faithfulness, having kept our first estate, we have been permitted to come into this world and receive tabernacles of flesh. The fact that we are living in the flesh is evidence that we did keep our first estate.

         —George Albert Smith

What is our relationship to God? The position that we stand in to him is that of a son. Adam is the father of our bodies, and God is the father of our spirits.

—John Taylor

Furthermore we have had fathers of our flesh which corrected us, and we gave them reverence: shall we not much rather be in subjection unto the Father of spirits, and live?

—Hebrews 12:9

The spirit, if it could be seen with mortal eyes, would appear in bodily shape like a full-grown person with individual endowments that make it a counterpart of the body in which it tabernacles, "that which is temporal in the likeness of that which is spiritual." (D & C 77:2.) It was that which came from God and entered at birth into the infant body prepared by its mortal parents. The spirit was of the "Lord from heaven." The physical body was "of the earth, earthy," (2 Cor. 15:47) or in other words, composed of the elements of which the things in the physical world are composed.

—Harold B. Lee

We are the offspring of God, begotten by him in the spirit world, where we partook of his nature as children here partake of the likeness of their parents.

—Lorenzo Snow

Then the word of the Lord came unto me, saying, Before I formed thee in the belly I knew thee; and before thou comest forth out of the womb I sanctified thee, and I ordained thee a prophet unto the nations.

—Jeremiah 1:4-5

And no man hath ascended up to heaven, but he that came down from heaven, even the Son of man which is in heaven.

—John 3:13

> Our birth is but a sleep and a forgetting;
> The Soul that rises with us, our life's star,
>   Hath had elsewhere its setting.
>   And cometh from afar;
>   Not in entire forgetfulness,
>   And not in utter nakedness,
> But trailing clouds of glory do we come
>   From God, who is our home:
>
> —William Wordsworth

I want to tell you, each and every one of you, that you are well acquainted with God our Heavenly Father, or the Great Elohim. You are all well acquainted with him, for there is not a soul of you but what has lived in his house and dwelt with him year after year; and yet you are seeking to become acquainted with him, when the fact is, you have merely forgotten what you did know....

There is not a person here today but what is a son or a daughter of that being. In the spirit world their spirits were first begotten and brought forth, and they lived there with their parents for ages before they came here.

—Brigham Young

Your father Abraham rejoiced to see my day: and he saw it, and was glad. Then said the Jews unto him, Thou art not yet fifty years old, and hast thou seen Abraham? Jesus said unto them, Verily, verily, I say unto you, Before Abraham was, I am.

—John 8:56-58

We are the children of God. He is the father of our spirits. We have not come from some lower form of life, but God is the Father of our spirits, and we belong to the royal family, because he is our father.

—George Albert Smith

Man is the offspring of God....We are as much the children of this great being as we are the children of our mortal progenitors. We are flesh of his flesh, bone of his bone, and the same fluid that circulates in our bodies, called blood, once circulated in his veins as it does in ours. As the seeds of grains, vegetables and fruits produce their kind, so man is in the image of God.

—Brigham Young

There were certain great principles involved in the organization of this earth, and one was that there might be a place provided whereon the children of our Heavenly Father could live and propagate their species and have bodies formed for the spirits to inhabit who were the children of God; for ... He is the God and Father of the spirits of all flesh.

—John Taylor

We believe that all men are the spirit children of God, created in his image. This concept is supported by the Holy Bible from Genesis to Revelation.

—Hugh B. Brown

We hear much nowadays as to the speculative ideas of men concerning the condition beyond the grave; but the admission that there is an individual existence beyond the grave, is a declaration that there must have been an individual, intelligent creation before we came here in the flesh. Life beyond the grave postulates a pre-existent state.

—James E. Talmage

We lived in the presence of God in the spirit before we came here. We desired to be like him, we saw him, we were in his presence. There is not a soul who has not seen both the Father and the Son, and in the spirit world we were in their presence, but it became necessary for us to gain experiences which could not be obtained in that world of spirits, and so we were accorded the privilege of coming down here upon this earth.

—Joseph Fielding Smith

We believe that we are the offspring of our Father in heaven, and that we possess in our spiritual organizations the same capabilities, powers and faculties that our Father possesses....

We are born in the image of God our Father; He begot us like unto Himself. There is the nature of Deity in the composition of our spiritual organization; in our spiritual birth our Father transmitted to us the capabilities, powers and faculties which He Himself possessed, as much so as the child on its mother's bosom possesses, although in an undeveloped state, the faculties, powers and susceptibilities of its parent.

—Lorenzo Snow

In the pre-existence we dwelt in the presence of God our Father. When the time arrived for us to be advanced in the scale of our existence and pass through this mundane probation, councils were held, and the spirit children were instructed in matters pertaining to conditions in mortal life, and the reason for such an existence. In the former life we were spirits. In order that we should advance and eventually gain the goal of perfection, it was made known that we would receive tabernacles of flesh and bones and have to pass through mortality where we would be tried and proved to see if we, by trial, would prepare ourselves for exaltation. We were made to realize, in the presence of our glorious Father, who had a tangible body of flesh and bones which shone like the sun, that we were, as spirits, far inferior in our station to him.

—Joseph Fielding Smith

It does seem strange that so many people doubt our divine ancestry, and that God is the Father of our spirits; yet from the very beginning, from the very earliest period of which we have any record in this world, He has been teaching men and women this fact....

When God created the earth and placed our first parents upon it, he did not leave them without knowledge concerning Himself. It is true that there had been taken from them the remembrance of their pre-existent life, but in His tender mercy He talked with them and later He sent His choice servants to instruct them in the things pertaining to eternal life.

—George Albert Smith

In the beginning was the Word, and the Word was with God, and the Word was God. The same was in the beginning with God.... And the Word was made flesh, and dwelt among us, (and we beheld his glory, the glory as of the only begotten of the Father,) full of grace and truth.

—John 1:1, 2, 14

That man has a spiritual body is evidenced by the account ... given in the writings of

Moses that man was created spiritually in heaven before he was given a natural body.

—J. Reuben Clark, Jr.

With regard to our position before we came here, ... we dwelt with the Father and with the Son, as expressed in the hymn, "O My Father." We dwelt in the presence of God before we came here.

—Wilford Woodruff

O My Father

O my Father, thou that dwellest
In the high and glorious place!
When shall I regain thy presence,
And again behold thy face?
In thy holy habitation,
Did my spirit once reside;
In my first primeval childhood,
Was I nurtured near thy side?

For a wise and glorious purpose
Thou hast placed me here on earth,
And withheld the recollection
Of my former friends and birth,
Yet ofttimes a secret something
Whispered, "You're a stranger here;"
And I felt that I had wandered
From a more exalted sphere.

I had learned to call thee Father,
Through thy Spirit from on high;
But until the key of knowledge

Was restored, I knew not why.
In the heavens are parents single?
No; the thought makes reason stare!
Truth is reason, truth eternal
Tells me I've a mother there.

When I leave this frail existence,
When I lay this mortal by,
Father, Mother, may I meet you
In your royal courts on high?
Then at length, when I've completed
All you sent me forth to do,
With your mutual approbation
Let me come and dwell with you.

—Eliza R. Snow

We say that God himself is a self-existent being. Who told you so? It is correct enough; but how did it get into your heads? Who told you that man did not exist in like manner upon the same principles? Man does exist upon the same principles. God made a tabernacle and put a spirit into it, and it became a living soul.

—Joseph Smith

What is the body without the spirit? It is lifeless clay. What is it that affects this lifeless clay? It is the spirit, it is the immortal part, the eternal being, that existed before it came here, that exists within us, and that will continue to exist and that by and by will redeem these tabernacles and bring them forth out of the grave.

—Joseph F. Smith

I am dwelling on the immortality of the spirit of man. Is it logical to say that the intelligence of spirits is immortal, and yet that it had a beginning? The intelligence of spirits had no beginning, neither will it have an end. That is good logic. That which has a beginning may have an end.

—Joseph Smith

Spirit is a substance ... it is material, but ... it is more pure, elastic and refined matter than the body ... it existed before the body, can exist in the body; and will exist separate from the body, when the body will be mouldering in the dust; and will, in the resurrection, be again united with it.

—Joseph Smith

For we know that if our earthly house of this tabernacle were dissolved, we have a building of God, an house not made with hands, eternal in the heavens.

—2 Corinthians 5:1

The spirit of man is not a created being; it existed from eternity and will exist to eternity. Anything created cannot be eternal; and earth, water, etc., had their existence in an elementary state, from eternity.

—Joseph Smith

The doctrine of pre-existence pours a wonderful flood of light upon the otherwise mysterious problem of man's origin. It shows that man, as a spirit, was begotten and born of heavenly parents and reared to maturity in the eternal mansions of the Father, prior to coming upon the earth in a temporal body to undergo an experience in mortality.

—Heber J. Grant

CHAPTER THREE
Our Earth Life

Earth Life with its joys and sorrows is a necessary part of our eternal existence. Its purposes are to prepare us to return to the presence of our Heavenly Father and to provide the way whereby we may receive a fulness of joy.

The principle of eternal progression and eternal happiness is dependent upon obtaining a physical body. Even the Savior of the world, the Only Begotten Son of God, was obliged to come to earth and to take upon himself an earthly tabernacle. He experienced joy and sorrow, happiness and grief, lasting satisfaction and frequent disappointments. As Paul has written, "Though he were a Son yet learned he obedience by the things which he suffered; and being made perfect, he became the author of eternal salvation unto all them that obey him."

John declared that "Christ received not of the fulness at the first," but that he "continued from grace to grace until he received a fullness and thus he was called the Son of God, because he received not of the fulness at the first."

Thus is it with us all. We must work out our salvation and exaltation by coming to this earth and receiving a physical body. If either we or the Savior could have attained unto our eternal exaltation without passing through the experiences of mortality, there would have been no purpose in our coming to earth. But this *was not possible. Man must be born into mortality and live and die that he may continue in his progress toward eternal life and exaltation.*

It is the wish of our Heavenly Father to bring all His children back into His presence. The spirits of all the human family dwelt with Him before they took tabernacles of flesh and became subject to the fall and to sin. He is their spiritual Father and has sent them here to be clothed with flesh and to be subject, with their tabernacles, to the ills that afflict fallen humanity. When they have proved themselves faithful in all things, and worthy before Him, they can then have the privilege of returning again to His presence, with their bodies to dwell in the abodes of the blessed. If man could have been made perfect, in his double capacity of body and spirit, without passing through the ordeals of mortality, there would have been no necessity of our coming into this state of trial and suffering. Could the Lord have glorified His children in spirit without a body like His own, He no doubt would have done so.

—Brigham Young

The object of our being placed upon this earth is that we may work out an exaltation, that we may prepare ourselves to go back and dwell with our Heavenly Father; and our Father, knowing the faults and failings of men has given us certain commandments to obey, and if we will examine those requirements and the things that devolve upon us we will find that they are all for our individual benefit and advancement. The school of life in which we are placed and the lessons that are given to us by our Father will make of us exactly what He desires, so that we may be prepared to dwell with Him.

—Heber J. Grant

This world is the state of our probation, and we look forward to the future as something with which we are as much connected as we are with anything pertaining to time. We look forward to another state of existence with that degree of certainty and confidence that we do when we go to bed in the evening expecting to see the light of the sun in the morning, or that we do with anything else that is associated with any of the affairs of this world upon which we place any degree of certainty. Were it not so, it would be, as I have already stated, of very little importance what our struggles were, or what we had to do with in this world.

—John Taylor

The boy, like to his father grown,
Has but attained unto his own;
To grow to sire from state of son,
Is not 'gainst Nature's course to run.
A son of God, like God to be,
Would not be robbing Deity;
And he who has this hope within,
Will purify himself from sin.
You're right, St. John, supremely right:
Who'er essays to climb this height,

Will cleanse himself of sin entire—
Or else 'twere needless to aspire.

—Lorenzo Snow

Man is a dual being possessed of body and spirit, made in the image of God and connected with him and with eternity. He is a God in embryo and will live and progress throughout the eternal ages, if obedient to the laws of the Godhead, as the Gods progress throughout the eternal ages.

—John Taylor

It has been decreed by the Almighty that spirits, upon taking bodies, shall forget all they had known previously, or they could not have a day of trial—could not have an opportunity for proving themselves in darkness and temptation, in unbelief and wickedness, to prove themselves worthy of eternal existence.

—Brigham Young

We are here for the purpose of redeeming and regenerating the earth on which we live, and God has placed his authority and his counsels here upon the earth for that purpose, that men may learn to do the will of God on the earth as it is done in heaven. This is the object of our existence.

—John Taylor

We have learned that we existed with God in eternity before we came into this life, and that we kept our estate. Had we not kept what is called our first estate and observed the laws that governed there, you and I would not be here today. We are here because we are worthy to be here, and that arises, to a great extent at least, from the fact that we kept our first estate.

—Lorenzo Snow

We came to this earth that we might have a body and present it pure before God in the celestial kingdom. The great principle of happiness consists in having a body. The devil has no body, and herein is his punishment. He is pleased when he can obtain the tabernacle of man, and when Cast out by the Savior he asked to go into the herd of swine, showing that he would prefer a swine's body to having none.

—Joseph Smith

We have come to sojourn in the flesh, to obtain tabernacle for our immortal spirits .... The object of our earthly existence is that we might have a fulness of joy and that we may become the sons and daughters of God, in the fullest sense of the word, being heirs of God and joint heirs with Jesus Christ, to be kings and priests unto God, to inherit glory, dominion, exaltation, thrones, and every power and attribute developed and possessed by our Heavenly Father. This is the object of our being on this earth.

—Joseph F. Smith

I sometimes wonder if people realize the purpose of their existence and the importance of the labor that men and women are expected to perform while on the earth....

We have been placed here for a purpose. That purpose is that we may overcome the evil temptations that are placed in our way, that we may learn to be charitable to one another, that we may overcome the passions with which we are beset, so that when the time comes for us to go to the other side we may be worthy, by reason of the effort we have put forth, to enjoy the blessings that our Father has in store for the faithful.

—George Albert Smith

It has been decreed by the Almighty that spirits, upon taking bodies, shall forget all they had known previously, or they could not have a day of trial—could not have an opportunity for proving themselves in darkness and temptation, in unbelief and wickedness, to prove themselves worthy of eternal existence.

—Brigham Young

We are here for the purpose of redeeming and regenerating the earth on which we live, and God has placed his authority and his counsels here upon the earth for that purpose, that men may learn to do the will of God on the earth as it is done in heaven. This is the object of our existence.

—John Taylor

We have learned that we existed with God in eternity before we came into this life, and that we kept our estate. Had we not kept what is called our first estate and observed the laws that governed there, you and I would not be here today. We are here because we are worthy to be here, and that arises, to a great extent at least, from the fact that we kept our first estate.

—Lorenzo Snow

We have come to sojourn in the flesh, to obtain tabernacle for our immortal spirits....The object of our earthly existence is that we might have a fulness of joy and that we may become the sons and daughters of God, in the fullest sense of the word, being heirs of God and joint heirs with Jesus Christ, to be kings and priests unto God, to inherit glory, dominion, exaltation, thrones, and every power and attribute developed and possessed by our Heavenly Father. This is the object of our being on this earth.

—Joseph F. Smith

I sometimes wonder if people realize the purpose of their existence and the importance of the labor that men and women are expected to perform while on the earth....

We have been placed here for a purpose. That purpose is that we may overcome the evil temptations that are placed in our way, that we may learn to be charitable to one another, that we may overcome the passions with which we are beset, so that when the time comes for us to go to the other side we may be worthy, by reason of the effort we have put forth, to enjoy the blessings that our Father has in store for the faithful.

—George Albert Smith

It is absolutely necessary that we should come to the earth and take upon us tabernacles; because if we did not have tabernacles we could not be like God or like Jesus Christ. God has a tabernacle of flesh and bone. He is an organized being just as we are, who are now in the flesh. Jesus Christ... had a fleshly tabernacle; He was crucified on the cross; and His body was raised from the dead....We are precisely in the same condition and under the same circumstances that God our Heavenly Father was when He was passing through this or a similar ordeal. We are destined to come forth out of the grave as Jesus did, and to obtain immortal bodies as He did....This is the object of our existence in the world.

—Joseph F. Smith

The object of man's taking a body is that through the redemption of Jesus Christ both soul and body may be exalted in the eternal world, when the earth shall be celestial, and obtain a higher exaltation than it would be possible for them to enjoy without these.... God had a purpose, therefore, in the organization of this earth, and in the placing of man upon it, and He has never deviated one hair to the right or to the left in regard to man and his destiny from that time until the present.

—John Taylor

One of the beautiful things to me in the gospel of Jesus Christ is that it brings us all to a common level. It is not necessary for a man to be a president of a stake or a member of the Quorum of the Twelve, in order to attain a high place in the celestial kingdom. The humblest member of the Church, if he keeps the commandments of God, will obtain an exaltation just as much as any other man in the celestial kingdom. The beauty of the gospel of Jesus Christ is that it makes us all equal in as far as we keep the commandments of the Lord. In as far as we observe to keep the laws of the Church we have equal opportunities for exaltation.

—George Albert Smith

CHAPTER FOUR
Death Comes To All

It is in the plan that man should die. The rich, the poor; the bond, the free; the great, the lowly—all must die. Death comes to everyone. Death is a necessary step to our eternal progression. But death is not the end, it is only a transitional state whereby we move from one stage of action to another. The spirit continues to live, move, think, learn, and to engage in all those activities associated with existence in our next estate. The physical body is placed in the grave, there to remain until the time of our resurrection.

The change called death is ordained of God and is a blessing to man. It would be tragic if men could never be released from mortality that they might put on immortality. Death releases man from his mortal existence and makes possible his onward progress toward eternal life and exaltation.

We are born to die, it is the inevitable end of all flesh, it being a fixed, unalterable decree of the Almighty concerning the human family.

—Joseph F. Smith

It would be tragic if a man, when he grew to be old were compelled to remained distressed and helpless in mortality, continuing on and on without the ability to enjoy longer life here. And so the Lord has decreed that we all come into the world in the same way, our time here being limited. We all have an opportunity to enjoy happiness in mortality, and then, if we have been wise, we pass on prepared for eternal happiness in the celestial kingdom when this earth shall be cleansed and purified by fire and will be presided over by our Heavenly Father and by our Elder Brother, Jesus Christ, as one of their dominions. With that assurance in our lives, death is not such a serious matter.

—George Albert Smith

Death has no real terror to any true Latter-day Saint. A true, faithful Latter-day Saint has been blessed with testimonies of the divinity of the work in which we are engaged, and he knows that when he passes to the other side he will have an eternity of joy and happiness.

—Heber J. Grant

There is no cause to fear death; it is but an incident in life. It is as natural as birth. Why should we fear it? Some fear it because they think it is the end of life, and life often is the dearest thing we have. Eternal life is man's greatest blessing.

If only men would "do his will" instead of looking hopelessly at the dark and gloomy tomb, they would turn their eyes heavenward and know that "Christ is risen!"

With all my soul I know that death is conquered by Jesus Christ.

—David O. McKay

It is true, we do not like to lose a good, kind companion, a wife, a husband, a child, a brother, a sister, or any of our near and dear friends or relatives; but we have to do it, and it is right and proper that we should. They go a little before us; when we get there they will receive and welcome us and say, "God bless you, you have come at last." That is the way I look at it. I expect to strike hands and embrace my friends who have gone before.

—John Taylor

Our friend and we were invited abroad on a party of pleasure, which is to last forever. His chair was ready first, and he has gone before us. We could not all conveniently start together; and why should you and I be grieved at this, since we are soon to follow, and know where to find him.

—Benjamin Franklin

We mourn; we sorrow for our loved ones that go—our wives, our husbands, our children, our parents; we sorrow for them; and it is well and proper that we should mourn for them and shed tears for the loss, for it is our loss; but it is their gain, for it is in the march of progress, advancement and development. It will be all right when our time comes, when we have finished our work and accomplished what the Lord required of us. If we are prepared, we need not be afraid to go, for it will be one of the most pleasant sensations that ever comes to the soul of man, whenever he departs, if he can go with a clear conscience into the presence of the Lord.

—Francis M. Lyman

We shall turn round and look upon it (the valley of death) and think, when we have crossed it, why this is the greatest advantage of my whole existence, for I have passed from a state of sorrow, grief, mourning, woe, misery, pain, anguish and disappointment into a state of existence, where I can enjoy life to the fullest extent as far as that can be done without a body. My spirit is set free, I thirst no more, I want to sleep no more, I tire no more, I run, I walk, I labor, I go, I come, I do this, I do that, whatever is required of me, nothing like pain or weariness, I am full of life, full of vigor, and I enjoy the presence of my Heavenly Father.

—Brigham Young

As a fond mother, when the day is o'er,
Leads by the hand her little child to bed,
Half willing, half reluctant to be led,
And leave his broken playthings on the floor,
Still gazing at them through the open door,

Nor wholly reassured and comforted
By promises of others in their stead,
Which, the more splendid, may not please him more;
So Nature deals with us, and takes away
Our playthings one by one, and by the hand
Leads us to rest so gently, that we go
Scarce knowing if we wish to go or stay,
Being too full of sleep to understand
How far the unknown transcends the what we know.
                                    —Henry W. Longfellow

Whether the spirit remains in the body a minute, an hour, a day, a year, or lives there until the body has reached a good old age, it is certain that the time will come when they (the spirit and the body) will be separated, and the body will return to mother earth, there to sleep upon that mother's bosom. That is all there is about death.
                                    —Brigham Young

Be of good cheer about death, and know this as a truth, that no evil can happen to a good man, either in life or after death.
                                    —Socrates

Death is the golden key that opens the palace of eternity.
                                    —John Milton

Be like a bird
That pausing in her flight
Awhile on boughs to light,

Feels them give way
Beneath her and yet sings,
Knowing that she hath wings.

—Victor Hugo

So live, that when thy summons comes to join
The innumerable caravan, that moves
To that mysterious realm, where each shall take
His chamber in the silent halls of death,
Thou go not, like the quarry-slave at night,
Scourged to his dungeon, but, sustained and soothed
By an unfaltering trust, approach thy grave,
Like one who wraps the drapery of his couch
About him, and lies down to pleasant dreams.

—William Cullen Bryant

We watch the liner in the distance glide
Out from the sheltered waters of the bay,
Into the arms of ocean's vastness won.
Enfolded in infinity of tide
We lose it, and the last faint smoke line gray
Merges into the sunset and is gone.

Vanished from sight and lost, art thou, at sea,
Swallowed in ocean's blue immensity?
Ah, no. Though trackless be the deep, and wide,
Thy pilot shall bring thee triumphantly
Into the harbor on the other side.

—Edith G. McGee

There is a great directing head of things and people—a supreme being, who looks after the destinies of the world. I have faith in a supreme being, and all my thoughts are regarding the life after death—where the soul goes, what form it takes and its relations to those now living.

I am convinced that the body is made up of entities which are intelligent. When one cuts his finger, I believe it is the intelligence of those entities that heals the wound. When one is sick, it is the intelligence of these entities that brings convalescence.

You know that there are living cells in the body so tiny that the microscope cannot show them at all. The entity that gives life and motion to the human body is finer still and lies infinitely beyond the reach of our finest scientific instruments. When this entity deserts the body, the body is like a ship without a rudder—deserted, motionless, dead.

—Thomas A. Edison

One may live as a conqueror, a king, or a magistrate; but he must die a man. The bed of death brings every human being to his pure individuality, to the intense contemplation of that deepest and most solemn of all relations—the relations between the creature and his Creator.

—Daniel Webster

How well he fell asleep!
Like some proud river, widening toward the sea;
   Calmly and grandly, silently and deep,
Life joined eternity.

—Samuel T. Coleridge

And so for me there is no sting of death,
    And so the grave has lost its victory.
It is but crossing—with abated breath
    And white, set face——a little strip of sea
To find the loved ones waiting on the shore,
    More beautiful, more precious than before.
                  —Ella Wheeler Wilcox

Oh, death, if thou a being art, draw near,
And let me clasp thee, for I hold thee dear.
I shall extort eternal life from thee;
Thou canst but grasp this wornout dress from me.
                  —Author Unknown

It is impossible that anything so natural, so necessary, and so universal as death should ever have been designed as an evil to mankind.
                  —Jonathan Swift

Living is death; dying is life—On this side of the grave we are exiles, on that, citizens; on this side, orphans; on that, children; on this side captives; on that freemen; on this side, disguised, unknown; on that, disclosed and proclaimed as the sons of God.
                  —Henry Ward Beecher

This world is the land of the dying; the next is the land of the living.
                  —Tryon Edwards

What is our death but a night's sleep? For as through sleep all weariness and faintness pass away and cease and powers of the spirit come back again, so that in the morning we arise fresh and strong and joyous; so at the Last Day we shall rise again as if we had only slept a night, and shall be fresh and strong.

—Martin Luther

The Lord gave, and the Lord hath taken away; blessed be the name of the Lord.

—Job 1:21

Some labor this side of the veil, others on the other side of the veil. If we tarry here we expect to labor in the cause of salvation and if we go hence we expect to continue our work until the coming of the Son of Man. The only difference is, while we are here we are subject to pain and sorrow, while they on the other side are free from affliction of every kind.

—Wilford Woodruff

When mourning the loss of our departed friends, I cannot help but think that in every death there is a birth; the spirit leaves the body dead to us, and passes to the other side of the veil alive to that great and noble company that are also working for the accomplishment of the purpose of God, in the redemption and salvation of a fallen world.

—Wilford Woodruff

I have been with Elders who died in the mission field, and a moment or two before they departed this life their faces have been overspread with a gleam of recognition of beings not of this world; they have uttered the names of loved ones long since gone and then have peacefully gone to their eternal rest.

—Charles A. Callis

The nearer I approach the end, the clearer I hear around me the immortal symphonies of the worlds which invite me. It is marvelous yet simple. For half a century I have been writing my thoughts in prose, verse, history, drama, romance, tradition, satire, ode and song–I have tried all; but I feel that I have not said a thousandth part of that which is in me. When I go down to the grave I can say like many others, "I have finished my day's work" but I cannot say, "I have finished my life's work"; my day's work will begin the next morning. The tomb is not a blind alley. It is an open thoroughfare. It closes in the twilight to open in the dawn. My work is only beginning; my work is hardly above its foundation. I would gladly see it mounting forever. The thirst for the infinite proves infinity.

—Victor Hugo

No man can pass into eternity, for he is already in it.

—Frederick W. Farrar

Sunset and evening star,
    And one clear call for me.
And may there be no moaning of the bar,
    When I put out to sea,

But such a tide as moving seems asleep,
    Too full for sound and foam,
When that which drew from out the boundless deep
    Turns again home.

Twilight and evening bell,
    And after that the dark!
And may there be no sadness of farewell,
    When I embark;

For though from out our bourne of Time and Place
    The flood may bear me far,
I hope to see my Pilot face to face
When I have crossed the bar.

                —Alfred Tennyson

We the living, should not think of the dead as lonely because if they could speak to us, they would say: "Do not weep for me, earth was not my true country, I was an alien there: I am at Home where everyone comes."

                —Helen Keller

I care not whether I am dying or not; for if I die I shall be with God; if I live, He will be with me.

                —Author Unknown

We call it death to leave this world, but were we once out of it, and enstated into the happiness of the next, we should think it were dying indeed to come back to it again.

—Sherlock

We picture death as coming to destroy; let us rather picture Christ as coming to save. We think of death as ending; let us rather think of life as beginning and that more abundantly. We think of losing; let us think of gaining. We think of parting, let us think of arriving. We think of going away; let us think of meeting. And as the voice of death whispers "You must go from earth," let us hear the voice of Christ saying, "You are but coming to me!"

—N. Macleo

In many places in the Scriptures, the separation of the body and spirit is called death; but that is not death in the strict sense of the term; that is only a change. We are naturally inclined to cling to our mother earth; our bodies love to live here, to see, to hear, to breathe, and to enjoy themselves because we are of the earth, earthy. But probably, in most cases, the change from mortal to immortality is no greater, comparatively speaking, than when a child emerges into this world. We shall suffer no more in putting off this flesh and leaving the spirit houseless than the child, in its capacity, does in its first efforts to breathe the breath of this mortal life.

—Brigham Young

Cowards die many times before their deaths:
The valiant never taste of death but once.
    Of all the wonders that I yet have heard,
It seems to me most strange that men should fear;
Seeing that death, a necessary end,
Will come when it will come.
                                —William Shakespeare

I cannot say, and I will not say
That he is dead.—He is just away!

With a cheery smile, and a wave of the hand,
He has wandered into an unknown land,
And left us dreaming how very fair
It needs must be, since he lingers there.

And you—O you, who the wildest yearn
For the old-time step and the glad return,—

Think of him faring on, as dear
In the love of There as the love of Here.

Think of him still as the same, I say:
He is not dead—he is just away!
                                —James Whitcomb Riley

We come here and sojourn in the flesh a little season, and then we pass away. Every soul that is born into the world will die. There is not a soul that has escaped death, except those upon whom God has passed by the power of His Spirit, that they should live in the flesh until the second coming of the Son of Man: but they will eventually have to pass through the ordeal called death; it may be in the twinkling of an eye, and without pain or suffering; but they will pass through the change, because it is an irrevocable edict of the Almighty. "In the day that thou eatest thou shall surely die."

This was the edict of the Almighty, and it pertains to Adam—that is, all the human race; for Adam is many, and it means you and me and every soul that lives and that bears the image of the Father. We shall all die.

—Joseph F. Smith

I suppose while we are mourning the loss of our friend, others are rejoicing to meet him behind the veil; and while he has left us, others are coming into the world at the same time, and probably in this our territory. There is a continuous change, an ingress of beings into the world and an egress out of it.

—John Taylor

Children are taken away in their infancy, and they go to the spirit world. They come here and fulfill the object of their coming, that is, they tabernacle in the flesh. They come to receive a probation and an inheritance on the earth; they obtain a body or tabernacle, and that tabernacle will be preserved for them, and in the morning of the resurrection the spirits and bodies will be reunited, and as here we find children of various ages in a family, from the infant at the mother's breast to manhood, so will it be in the family organization in the celestial world. Our children will be restored to us as they are laid down if we, their parents, keep the faith and prove ourselves worthy to obtain eternal life; and if we do not so prove ourselves our children will still be preserved, and will inherit celestial glory.

—Wilford Woodruff

The Lord takes many away, even in infancy, that they may escape the envy of man, and the sorrows and evils of this present world; they were too pure, too lovely, to live on earth; therefore if rightly considered, instead of mourning we have reason to rejoice as they are delivered from evil, and we shall soon have them again.

—Joseph Smith

I will say to our mourning friends, your children are taken away and you cannot help it; we cannot any of us help it; there is no censure to be given to parents when they do the best they can. A mother should not be censured because she cannot save her sick child and we have to leave these things in the hands of God.

—Wilford Woodruff

Unanswered yet? That prayer your lips have pleaded?
In agony of heart these many years?
Does faith begin to fail; is hope departing,
And think you all in vain those falling tears?
Say not the Father has not heard your prayer;
You shall have your desire sometime, somewhere.

Unanswered yet? Though when you first presented
This one petition at the Father's throne,

It seemed you could not wait the time of asking,
So urgent was your heart to make it known.
Though years have passed since then, do not despair;
The Lord will answer you sometime, somewhere.

Unanswered yet? Nay, do not say ungranted;
Perhaps your own part is not yet wholly done,
The work began when first your prayer was uttered.
And God will finish what he has begun.
If you will keep the incense burning there,
His glory you shall see sometime, somewhere.

Unanswered yet? Faith cannot be unanswered;
Her feet were firmly planted on the Rock;
Amid the wildest storms she stands undaunted,
Nor quails before the loudest thunder shock
She knows Omnipotence has heard her prayer,
And cries, "It shall be done," sometime, somewhere.
                              —Ophelia G. Adams

Heaven gives its favorites early death.

                                   —Byron

Good-night! good-night! as we so oft have said,
    Beneath this roof at midnight, in the days
    That are no more, and shall no more return.
Thou hast but taken up thy lamp and gone to bed;
I stay a little longer, as one stays
    To cover up the embers that still buRN.
                          —Henry W. Longfellow

There are some things which have not been
revealed to man, but are held in the bosom

of God our Father, and it may be that the condition after death of those who die in infancy is among the things which God has never revealed; but it is sufficient for me to know that our children are saved, and that if we ourselves keep the faith and do our duty before the Lord, if we keep the celestial law, we shall be preserved by the law, and our children will be given unto us there, as they have been given here in this world of sorrow, affliction, pain and distress.

—Wilford Woodruff

Every man born into the world will die. It matters not where he is, whether his birth be among the rich and the noble, or among the lowly and poor in the world, his days are numbered with the Lord, and in due time he will reach the end. We should think of this. Not that we should go about with heavy hearts or with downcast countenance; not at all.

I rejoice that I am born to live, to die, and to live again. I thank God for this intelligence. It gives me joy and peace that the world cannot give, neither can the world take it away. God has revealed this to me, in the Gospel of Jesus Christ. I know it to be true. Therefore, I have nothing to be sad over, nothing to make me sorrowful. All that I have to do with in the world is calculated to buoy me up, to give me joy and peace, hope and consolation in this present life, and a glorious hope of salvation and exaltation in the presence of my God in the world to come. I have no reason to mourn, not even at death.

It is true, I am weak enough to weep at the death of my friends and kindred. I may shed tears when I see the grief of others. I have sympathy in my soul for the children of men. I can weep with them when they weep; I can rejoice with them when they rejoice; but I have no cause to mourn, nor to be sad because death comes into the world. I am speaking now of the temporal death, the death of the body. All fear of this death has been removed from the Latter-day Saints. They have no dread of the temporal death, because they know that as death came upon them by the transgression of Adam, so by the righteousness of Jesus Christ shall life come unto them, and though they die, they shall live again. Possessing this knowledge they have joy even in death, for they know that they shall rise again and shall meet again beyond the grave.

—Joseph F. Smith

> There is no flock, however watched and tended,
>   But one dead lamb is there!
> There is no fireside, howsoe'er defended,
>   But has one vacant chair!

—Longfellow

The day which you fear as being the end of all things is the birthday of your eternity.

—Seneca

God in his eternal decrees, has ordained that all men must die, but as to the mode and manner of our exit...it matters very little.

—John Taylor

Supposing I live, I have got a work to do; and if I die, I shall still be engaged in the cause of Zion...If we live, we live to God; and if we die, we die to God; and we are God's, any way.

—John Taylor

The only difference between the old and young dying is, one lives longer in heaven and eternal light and glory than the other, and is freed a little sooner from this miserable wicked world.

—Joseph Smith

I regret ofttimes, in the times of distress and trouble that come to those whom we admire and love, that we are not able to lift from their shoulders the sorrow into which they are plunged, when they are called upon to part with those they cherish.

But we realize that our Father in heaven can bind up broken hearts and that He can dispel sorrow and that He can point forward with joy and satisfaction to those blessings that are to come through obedience to the Gospel of the Lord Jesus Christ, for we do understand and we do have conviction that it is the will of our Father in heaven that we shall live on and that we have not finished our existence when these bodies of mortality are laid away in the grave.

It is a very great blessing that in the providence of the Lord and in the revelations that have been given by our Father in heaven, we have the assurance that the spirit and the body, in due time, will be reunited, not withstanding the unbelief that there is in the world today—and there certainly is great skepticism and unbelief in relation to this matter. But notwithstanding this we have assurance through the revelations that have been given by the Lord our God, that that is the purpose of God, that the body and the spirit shall be eternally united and that there will come a time, through the blessing and mercy of God, when we will no more have sorrow but when we shall have conquered all of these things that are of a trying and distressing character, and shall stand up in the presence of the living God, filled with joy and peace and satisfaction.

I was thoroughly convinced in my own mind and in my own heart, when my first wife left me by death, that it was the will of the Lord that she should be called away. I bowed in humility at her death. The Lord saw fit upon that occasion to give to one of my little children a testimony that the death of her mother was the will of the Lord.

About one hour before my wife died, I called my children into her room and told them that their mother was dying and for them to bid her goodbye. One of the little girls, about twelve years of age, said to me: "Papa, I do not want my mamma to die. I have been with you in the hospital in San Francisco for six months; time and time again when Mamma was in distress you have administered to her and she has been relieved of her pain and quietly gone to sleep. I want you to lay hands upon my mamma and heal her."

I told my little girl that we all had to die sometime and that I felt assured in my heart that her mother's time had arrived; and she and the rest of the children left the room.

I knelt down by the bed of my wife (who by this time had lost consciousness) and I told the Lord I acknowledged His hand in life, in death, in joy, in sorrow, in prosperity or adversity; I thanked Him for the knowledge I had that my wife belonged to me for all eternity, that the Gospel of Jesus Christ had been restored, that I knew that by the power and authority of the Priesthood here on earth that I could and would have my wife forever if I were only faithful as she has been; but I told the Lord that I lacked the strength to have my wife die and to have it affect the faith of my little children in the ordinances of the Gospel of Jesus Christ; and I supplicated the Lord with all the strength that I possessed, that He would give to that little girl of mine a knowledge that it was His mind and His will that her Mamma should die.

Within an hour my wife passed away, and I called the children back into the room. My little boy about five and a half years of age was weeping bitterly, and the little girl twelve years of age took him in her arms and said: "Do not weep, the voice of the Lord from heaven has said to me, 'In the death of your mamma the will of the Lord shall be done.'"

Tell me, my friends, that I do not know that God hears and answers prayers! Tell me that I do not know that in the hour of adversity the Latter-day Saints are comforted and blessed and consoled as no other people are!

I have been blessed with only two sons. One of them died at five years of age and the other at seven. My last son died of a hip disease. I had built great hopes that he would live to spread the Gospel at home and abroad and be an honor to me. About an hour before he died I had a dream that his mother, who was dead, came for him, and that she brought with her a messenger, and she told this messenger to take the boy while I was asleep; and in the dream I thought I awoke and I succeeded in getting him away from the messenger who had come to take him, and in so doing I dreamed that I stumbled and fell upon him.

I dreamed that I fell upon his sore hip, and the terrible cries and anguish of the child drove me nearly wild. I could not stand it and I jumped up and ran out of the house so as not to hear his distress. I dreamed that after running out of the house I met Brother Joseph E. Taylor and told him of these things.

He said: "Well, Heber, do you know what I would do if my wife came for one of her children–I would not struggle for that child; I would not oppose her taking that child away. If a mother who had been faithful had passed beyond the veil, she would know of the suffering and the anguish her child may have to suffer; she would know whether that child might go through life as a cripple and whether it would be better or wiser for that child to be relieved from the torture of life; and when you stop to think, Brother Grant, that the mother of that boy went down into the shadow of death to give him life, she is the one who ought to have the right to take him or keep him."

I said, "I believe you are right, Brother Taylor, and if she comes again, she shall have the boy without any protest on my part."

After coming to that conclusion, I was waked by my brother, B.F. Grant, who was staying that night with us, helping to watch over the sick boy. He called me into the room and told me that my child was dying. I went in the front room and sat down. There was a vacant chair between me and my wife who is now living, and I felt the presence of that boy's deceased mother, sitting in that chair. I did not tell anybody what I felt, but I turned to my living wife and said: "Do you feel anything strange?" She said: "Yes, I feel assured that Heber's mother is sitting between us, waiting to take him away."

Now I am naturally, I believe, a sympathetic man. I was raised as an only child, with all the affection that a mother could lavish upon a boy. I believe that I am naturally affectionate and sympathetic and that I shed tears for my friends—tears of joy for their success and tears of sorrow for their misfortunes. But I sat by the deathbed of my little boy and saw him die without shedding a tear. My living wife, my brother, and I, upon that occasion experienced a sweet, peaceful and heavenly influence in my home as great as I have ever experienced in my life; and no person can tell me that every other Latter-day Saint that has a knowledge of the Gospel in his heart and soul, can really mourn for his loved ones, only in the loss of their society here in this life.

—Heber J. Grant

CHAPTER FIVE
Life in the Spirit World

What happens when one dies? The spirit leaves the body. Nothing is lost. True, the body has become lifeless. It has lost its power of movement. Its mouth can no longer speak. Its ears can no longer hear. Its feet can no longer run. The body is without life. A brief separation has taken place—the body remains, but the spirit has left its earthly habitation. One moment life is there and the next moment life is gone. When death comes the body is unable to continue its daily activities. Where has the life gone? The spirit, that which is the life of body, has gone into the spirit world.

What we call death is not an end to existence. The spirit at death has not lost any of its power. The body is still, but the spirit has gone to mingle with other spirits and to enjoy the association and company of other loved ones who have departed this life. The spirit is as much alive after death as it was in life or as it has been since it was begotten by its Heavenly Parents prior to its earthly existence.

The Prophet Joseph Smith taught that the spirits of our loved ones are not far from us after they die. They are near and anxious about us.

When men are prepared, they are better off to go hence.... The spirits of the just are exalted to a greater and more glorious work; hence they are blessed in their departure to the world of spirits.

Enveloped in flaming fire, they are not far from us, and know and understand our thoughts, feelings, and motions and are often pained therewith.

—Joseph Smith

When the spirits leave their bodies they are in the presence of our Father and God; they are prepared then to see, hear and understand spiritual things. But where is the spirit world? It is incorporated within this celestial system. Can you see it with your natural eyes? No. Can you see spirits in this room? No. Suppose the Lord should touch your eyes that you might see, could you then see the spirits? Yes, as plainly as you now see bodies, as did the servant of Elijah. If the Lord would permit it, and it was His will that it should be done, you could see the spirits that have departed from this world as plainly as you now see bodies with your natural eyes.

—Brigham Young

When a person, who has always been good and faithful to his God, lays down his body in the dust, his spirit will remain the same in the spirit world. It is not the body that has control over the spirit, as to its disposition, but it is the spirit that controls the body. When the spirit leaves the body the body becomes lifeless. The spirit has not changed one single particle of itself by leaving the body.

—Heber C. Kimball

Passing the veil does not alter a man; it certainly takes him from the eyes of flesh, but the capacity, the intelligence, the thinking powers, are all alive and quick; and if they hear the Gospel they will be glad, and the promises are made to them, and they will rejoice in them.

—Parley P. Pratt

As quickly as the spirit is unlocked from this house of clay, it is free to travel with lightning speed to any planet, or fixed star, or to the uttermost part of the earth, or to the depths of the sea, according to the will of Him who dictates.

—Brigham Young

Is the spirit world here? It is not beyond the sun, but is on this earth that was organized for the people that have lived and that do and will live upon it. No other people can have it, and we can have no other kingdom until we are prepared to inhabit this eternally.

—Brigham Young

Flesh and blood cannot go there (the spirit world); but flesh and bones, quickened by the Spirit of God, can.

—Joseph Smith

When a good man or woman dies, the spirit does not go to the sun or the moon...the spirits go to God who gave them....The moment your eyes are opened upon the spirit land, you will find yourselves in the presence of God, for as David says, "If I take the wings of the morning, and dwell to the uttermost parts of the sea;...thou art there; and if I make my bed in hell, behold thou art there." You are in the presence of God, and when your eyes are opened you will understand it.

—Brigham Young

If a man has knowledge, he can be saved; although, if he has been guilty of great sins, he will be punished for them. But when he consents to obey the Gospel, whether here or in the world of spirits, he is saved.

—Joseph Smith

I have a father, brothers, children, and friends who have gone to a world of spirits. They are only absent for a moment. They are in the spirit, and we shall soon meet again. The time will soon arrive when the trumpet shall sound. When we depart, we shall hail our mothers, fathers, friends, and all whom we love who have fallen asleep in Jesus. There will be no fear of mobs persecutions, or malicious law-suits and arrests; but it will be an eternity of felicity.

—Joseph Smith

We have more friends behind the veil than on this side, and they will hail us more joyfully than you were ever welcomed by your parents and friends in this world; and you will rejoice more when you meet them than you ever rejoiced to see a friend in this life; and then we shall go on from step to step, from rejoicing to rejoicing, and from one intelligence and power to another, our happiness becoming more and more exquisite and sensible as we proceed in the words and powers of life.

—Brigham Young

I refer to William McKay and Ellen Oman, as my grandparents, I refer to my father and mother, my brothers and sisters over there now.

I hope to meet them and recognize them and love them as I recognized and loved them here. And I base that upon knowledge that is as real as my speaking to you. It has come through inspiration from on high, and I base it also upon the biblical scripture that as Christ's body lay in the tomb his spirit went to preach to the spirits in prison which were disobedient at one time, in the days of Noah.

—David O. McKay

It is right that the ties should be strengthened between us and the spirit world. Everyone who departs from this mortal state of existence only adds another link to the chain of connection—another tie to draw us nearer to our Father and God, and to those intelligences which dwell in his presence.

—Brigham Young

Our fathers and mothers, brothers, sisters and friends who have passed away from this earth, having been faithful and worthy to enjoy these rights and privileges, may have a mission given them to visit their relatives and friends upon the earth again, bringing from the divine presence messages of love, of warning, of reproof and instruction to those whom they had learned to love in the flesh.

—Joseph F. Smith

I have been at the other side of the veil, in vision, and have seen a degree of its condition with the eyes that God gave me. I have seen it and have seen those that lived in the faith and had the privilege of seeing Jesus, Peter, James, and the rest of the ancient Apostles, and of hearing them preach the gospel. I have also seen those who rebelled against them, and they still had a rebellious spirit, fighting against God and his servants.

—Heber C. Kimball

I will say that this nation and all nations, together with presidents, kings, emperors, judges, and all men, righteous and wicked have got to go into the spirit world and stand before the bar of God. They have got to give an account of the deeds done in the body.

—Wilford Woodruff

I feel at liberty to reveal to this assembly this morning what has been revealed to me since we were here yesterday morning. If the veil could be taken from our eyes and we could see into the spirit world, we would see that Joseph Smith, Brigham Young and John Taylor had gathered together every spirit that ever dwelt in the flesh in this Church since its organization. We would also see the faithful apostles and elders of the Nephites who dwelt in the flesh in the days of Jesus Christ. In that assembly we would also see Isaiah and every prophet and apostle that ever prophesied of the great work of God. In the midst of these spirits we would see the Son of God, the Savior, who presides and guides and controls the preparing of the kingdom of God on the earth and in heaven. From that body of spirits, when we shout "Hosannah to God and the Lamb!" there is a mighty shout goes up of "Glory to God in the Highest!" that the God of Israel has permitted His people to finish his Temple and prepare it for the great work that lies before the Latter-day Saints. These patriarchs and prophets who have wished for this day, rejoice in the spirit world that the day has come when the Saints of the Most High God have had power to carry out this great mission.

—Wilford Woodruff

The faithful Elders who leave this world will preach to the spirits in the spirit world. In that world there are millions and millions to every Elder who leaves here, and yet every spirit will be preached to that has had a tabernacle on the earth and become accountable.

—Brigham Young

Those who have gone before us have something to do as well as we have here. They are laboring to prepare the inhabitants of the Spirit world for the coming of Christ, the same as we are trying to prepare the inhabitants of the earth for the same great event.

—Wilford Woodruff

Jesus himself set the example and pattern for others. While his body lay in the silent tomb, his noble spirit was not idle; hence, Peter says, that Jesus, being put to death in the flesh was quickened by the spirit, by which also he went and preached to the spirits in prison that were sometime disobedient in the days of Noah. Jesus entered the prison house of those persons who were destroyed in the mighty flood, and preached to them. Those antediluvian spirits had suffered in the prison some two thousand years, and upwards; they needed some information, and Jesus went to enlighten them.

—Orson Pratt

He [Willard Richards] has gone to the world of spirits to engage in a work he could not do if he had remained in the flesh. I do not believe he could have done as much work for the general good of the cause of God, had he remained in the flesh, as he can accomplish now in the spirit; for there is a work to do there—the Gospel to preach, Israel to gather that they may purify themselves, and become united in one heart and mind.

—Heber C. Kimball

Spirits can only be revealed in flaming fire or glory. Angels have advanced further, their light and glory being tabernacled; and hence they appear in bodily shape.

—Joseph Smith

Spirits are just as familiar with spirits as bodies are with bodies, though spirits are composed of matter so refined as not to be tangible to this coarser organization.

—Brigham Young

The spirits of our children are immortal before they come to us, and their spirits, after bodily death, are like they were before they came. They are as they would have appeared if they had lived in the flesh, to grow to maturity or to develop their physical bodies to the full stature of their spirits. If you see one of your children that has passed away it may appear to you in the form in which you would recognize it, the form of childhood; but if it came to you as a messenger bearing some important truth, it would perhaps come ... in the stature of full-grown manhood....

The Spirit of Jesus Christ was full-grown before he was born into the world; and so our children were full-grown and possessed their full stature in the spirit before they entered mortality, the same stature that they will possess after they have passed away from mortality, and as they will also appear after the resurrection, when they shall have completed their mission.

—Joseph F. Smith

Let a man pass the veil with the everlasting priesthood, having magnified it to the day of his death, and you cannot get it off him; it will remain with him in the world of spirits; and when he wakes up in that world among the spirits, he has that power and that obligation on him, that if he can find a person worthy of salvation, why, as soon as he ascertains that, and he remembers what he may teach and whom he may teach he then discovers that he has got a Mission, and that Mission is to those souls who had not the privilege which we have in this world, that they may be partakers of the Gospel as well as we.

—Parley P. Pratt

As soon as Joseph received the keys of the Aaronic and Melchizedek Priesthood, as soon as he received the keys from Moses for the gathering together of the house of Israel in the latter

days, and from Elijah to seal the hearts of the
fathers to the children and children to the fathers—
when Joseph received all these keys, and had power
to seal them upon the heads of other men, the Lord
called him away. Why did he call him into the spirit
world? Because he held the keys of this dispensa-
tion, not only before he came to this world and
while he was in the flesh, but he would hold them
throughout the endless ages of eternity. He held the
keys of past generations–of the millions of people
who dwelt on the earth in the fifty generations that
had passed and gone who had not the law of the
gospel, who never saw a prophet, never saw an
Apostle, never heard the voice of any man who was
inspired of God and had power to teach them the
gospel of Christ, and to organize the church of
Christ on earth. He went to unlock the prison
doors to these people, as far as they would receive
his testimony, and the Saints of God who dwell in
the flesh will build temples unto the name of the
Lord, and enter these temples and perform certain
ordinances for the redemption of the dead. This was
the work of Joseph the prophet in the spirit world.
Now, I believe in my own mind that every Elder of
Israel who has gone into the spirit world, who has
been faithful in the flesh, has as much to do on the
other side of the veil as we have to do here, and if
anything more so. This is my view with regard to
the labors of the Elders of Israel. The Lord hath
need of some on the other side of the veil. He pre-
serves some to labor here, and he takes whom he

will according to the counsels of his own will; this is his manner of dealing. Those of our brethren who have passed away have got through the labors of the flesh; we are left here to labor a little while on the earth.

—Wilford Woodruff

Jesus Christ became a ministering spirit (while His body was lying in the sepulcher) to the spirits in prison, to fulfill an important part of His mission, without which He could not have perfected His work, or entered into His rest.

—Joseph Smith

Now, among all these millions and thousands of millions of spirits that have lived in the earth and have passed away, from generation to generation, since the beginning of the world, without the knowledge of the gospel—among them you may count that at least one half are women. Who is going to preach the gospel to the women? Who is going to carry the testimony of Jesus Christ to the hearts of the women who have passed away without a knowledge of the gospel?

Well, to my mind, it is a simple thing. These good sisters have been set apart, ordained to the work, called to it, authorized by the authority of the Holy Priesthood to minister, for their sex, in the House of God for the living and for the dead, will be fully authorized and empowered to preach the gospel and minister to the women while the elders and prophets are preaching it to the men. The things we experience here are typical of the things of God and the life beyond us.

—Joseph F. Smith

I believe...that when the gospel is preached to the spirits in prison, the success attending that preaching will be far greater than that attending the preaching of our elders in this life. I believe there will be very few indeed of those spirits who will not gladly receive the gospel when it is carried to them. The circumstances there will be a thousand times more favorable.

—Lorenzo Snow

God hath made a provision that every spirit in the eternal world can be ferreted out and saved, unless he has committed that unpardonable sin which cannot be remitted to him either in this world or the world of spirits. God has wrought out a salvation for all men, unless they have committed a certain sin; and every man who has a friend in the eternal world can save him, unless he has committed the unpardonable sin. And so you can see how far you can be a savior.

—Joseph Smith

Compare those inhabitants on the earth who have heard the gospel in our day, with the millions who have never heard it, or had the keys of salvation presented to them, and you will conclude

at once as I do, that there is a mighty work to perform in the spirit world.

—Brigham Young

There is a connecting link between the priesthood in the heavens and the priesthood
upon the earth.

God, our Heavenly Father, has gathered unto
himself, through the atonement of Jesus Christ, very
many great and honorable men who have lived upon
the earth, and have been clothed with the powers of
the priesthood. Those men having held that priesthood and administered in it upon the earth are now
in the heavens operating with the priesthood in the
heavens in connection with the priesthood that
exists now upon the earth.

—John Taylor

Father Smith and Carlos and Brother
Partridge, yes, and every other good Saint,
are just as busy in the spirit world as you and I are
here. They can see us, but we cannot see them unless
our eyes are opened. What are they doing there?
They are preaching, preaching all the time, and
preparing the way for us to hasten our work in
building temples here and elsewhere, and to go back
to Jackson County and build the great temple of the
Lord. They are hurrying to get ready by the time we
are ready, and we are all hurrying to get ready by the
time our Elder Brother is ready.

—Brigham Young

I can say with regard to parting with our friends, and going ourselves, that I have been near enough to understand eternity so that I have had to exercise a great deal more faith to desire to live than I ever exercised in my whole life to live. The brightness and glory of the next apartment is inexpressible. It is not encumbered so that when we advance in years we have to be stubbing along and be careful lest we fall down. But yonder, how different! They move with ease and like lightning. If we want to visit Jerusalem, or this, that, or the other place—and I presume we will be permitted if we desire—there we are, looking at its streets. If we want to behold Jerusalem as it was in the days of the Savior; or if we want to see the Garden of Eden as it was when created, there we are, and we see it as it existed spiritually, for it was created first spiritually and then temporally, and spiritually it still remains. And when there we may behold the earth as at the dawn of creation, or we may visit any city we please that exists upon its surface. If we wish to understand how they are living here on these western islands, or in China, we are there; in fact, we are like the light of the morning, or, I will not say the electric fluid, but its operations on the wires. God has revealed some little things, with regard to his movements and power, and the operation and motion of the lightning furnish a fine illustration of the ability of the Almighty.

When we pass into the spirit world we shall possess a measure of his power. Here, we are continually troubled with ills and ailments of various kinds. In

the spirit world we are free from all this and enjoy
life, glory, and intelligence; and we have the Father
to speak to us, Jesus to speak to us, and angels to
speak to us, and we shall enjoy the society of the just
and the pure who are in the spirit world until the
resurrection.

—Brigham Young

I went to see him [Jedediah M. Grant] one day
last week, and he reached out his hand and
shook hands with me; he could not speak, but he
shook hands warmly with me....

I laid my hands upon him and blessed him, and
asked God to strengthen his lungs that he might be
easier, and in two or three minutes he raised himself
up and talked for about an hour as busily as he
could, telling me what he had seen and what he
understood, until I was afraid he would weary himself, when I arose and left him.

He said to me, brother Heber, I have been into
the spirit world two nights in succession, and, of all
the dreads that ever came across me, the worst was
to have to again return to my body, though I had to
do it. But O says he, the order of righteous men and
women; I beheld them organized in their several
grades, and there appeared to be no obstruction to
my vision; I could see every man and woman in
their grade and order. I looked to see whether there
was any disorder there, but there was none; neither
could I see any death nor any darkness, disorder or
confusion. He said that the people he there saw were

organized in family capacities; and when he looked at them he saw grade after grade, and all were organized and in perfect harmony. He would mention one item after another and say, "Why, it is just as brother Brigham says it is; it is just as he has told us many a time...."

He saw the righteous gathered together in the spirit world, and there were no wicked spirits among them. He saw his wife; she was the first person that came to him. He saw many that he knew, but did not have conversation with any except his wife Caroline. She came to him, and he said that she looked beautiful and had their little child, that died on the Plains, in her arms and said, "Mr. Grant, here is little Margaret; you know that the wolves ate her up, but it did not hurt her; here she is all right."

"To my astonishment," he said, "when I looked at families there was a deficiency in some, there was a lack, for I saw families that would not be permitted to be born and dwell together, because they had not honored their calling here."

He asked his wife Caroline where Joseph and Hyrum and Father Smith and others were; she replied, "they have gone away ahead, to perform and transact business for us." The same as when brother Brigham and his brethren left Winter Quarters and came here to search out a home; they came to find a location for their brethren.

He also spoke of the buildings he saw there, remarking that the Lord gave Solomon wisdom and poured gold and silver into his hands that he might display his skill and ability, and said that the temple erected by Solomon was much inferior to the most ordinary buildings he saw in the spirit world.

In regard to gardens, says brother Grant, "I have seen good gardens on this earth, but I never saw any to compare with those that were there. I saw flowers of numerous kinds, and some with from fifty to a hundred different colored flowers growing upon one stalk." We have many kinds of flowers on the earth, and I suppose those very articles came from heaven, or they would not be here.

After mentioning the things that he had seen, he spoke of how much he disliked to return and resume his body, after having seen the beauty and glory of the spirit world, where the righteous spirits are gathered together.

Some may marvel at my speaking about these things, for many profess to believe that we have no spiritual existence. But do you not believe that my spirit was organized before it came to my body here? And do you not think there can be houses and gardens, fruit trees, and every other thing there. The spirits of those things were made, as well as our spirits, and it follows that they can exist upon the same principle.

After speaking of the gardens and the beauty of every thing there, brother Grant said that he felt extremely sorrowful at having to leave so beautiful a place and come back to earth, for he looked upon his body with loathing, but was obliged to enter it again.

He said that after he came back he could look upon his family and see the spirit that was in them, and the darkness that was in them; and that he conversed with them about the gospel, and what they should do, and they replied, "Well, brother Grant, perhaps it is so, and perhaps it is not," and said that was the state of this people to a great extent, for many are full of darkness and will not believe me.

—Heber C. Kimball

CHAPTER SIX
The Resurrection

How empty life would seem if there were no resurrection! The declaration by the angel, "He is risen!" is a message filled with hope for every child of God. Job declared, "If a man die, shall he live again?" He answered his own question with a positive declaration that he knew that he would be resurrected and that in the flesh he would see God. It is marvelous to know from the testimony of the living prophets and from the appearance of resurrected beings that there is a resurrection and that we shall have the association of our friends and loved ones at a future time—to know that we shall know them there as we knew them here.

The appearance of the resurrected Savior to Mary Magdalene, the apostles, and others is the FIRST evidence of the resurrection among men. It is recorded that when Mary visited the tomb where Jesus had been buried she heard a voice say to her:

Woman, why weepest thou? whom seekest thou? She, supposing him to be the gardener, saith unto him, Sir, if thou have borne him hence, tell me where thou hast laid him, and I will take him away. Jesus saith unto her, Mary. She turned herself, and saith unto him, Rabboni; which is to say, Master. Jesus saith unto her, Touch me not; for I am not yet ascended to my Father: but go to my brethren, and say unto them, I ascend unto my Father, and your Father; and to my God, and your God....

Then the same day at evening, being the first day of the week, when the doors were shut where the disciples were assembled for fear of the Jews, came Jesus and stood in the midst, and saith unto them, Peace be unto you. And when he had so said, he shewed unto them his hands and his side. Then were the disciples glad, when they saw the Lord....

And after eight days again his disciples were within, and Thomas with them: then came Jesus, the doors being shut, and stood in the midst, and said, Peace be unto you. Then saith he to Thomas, Reach hither thy finger, and behold my hands; and reach hither thy hand, and thrust it into my side; and be not faithless, but believing. And Thomas answered and said unto him, My Lord and my God. Jesus saith unto him, Thomas, because thou hast seen me, thou hast believed: blessed are they that have not seen, and yet have believed.

—John 20:15-16, 17, 19, 20, 26-29

The resurrection of Jesus was the beginning of life beyond the grave. It is recorded that at the time of the Savior's resurrection, the graves were opened; and many bodies of the saints which slept arose, And came out of the graves after his resurrection, and went into the holy city, and appeared unto many.

—Matt. 27:52-53

Matthew recorded the resurrection of Christ as follows:

And the angel answered and said unto the women, Fear not ye: for I know that ye seek Jesus, which was crucified. He is not here: for he is risen, as he said. Come, see the place where the Lord lay. And go quickly, and tell his disciples that he is risen from the dead; and, behold, he goeth before you into Galilee; there shall ye see him: lo, I have told you.... And as they went to tell his disciples, behold, Jesus met them, saying, All hail. And they came and held him by the feet, and worshipped him....Then the eleven disciples went away into Galilee, into a mountain where Jesus had appointed them. And when they saw him, they worshipped him: but some doubted. And Jesus came and spake unto them, saying, All power is given unto me in heaven and in earth.

—Ibid., 28:5-7, 9, 16-18

But as touching the resurrection of the dead, have ye not read that which was spoken unto you by God, saying, I am the God of Abraham, and the God of Isaac, and the God of Jacob? God is not the God of the dead, but of the living.

—Ibid., 22:31, 32

The spirit and the body shall be reunited again in its perfect form; both limb and joint shall be restored to its proper frame, even as we now are at this time; and we shall be brought to stand before God, knowing even as we know now, and have a bright recollection of all our guilt.

Now, this restoration shall come to all, both old and young, both bond and free, both male and female, both the wicked and the righteous; and even there shall not so much as a hair of their heads be lost; but everything shall be restored to its perfect frame, as it is now, or in the body, and shall be brought and be arraigned before the bar of Christ the Son, and God the Father, and the Holy Spirit, which is one Eternal God, to be judged according to their works, whether they be good or whether they be evil.

Now, behold, I have spoken unto you concerning the death of the mortal body, and also concerning the resurrection of the mortal body. I say unto you that this mortal body is raised to an immortal body, that is from death, even from the first death unto life, that they can die no more; their spirits uniting with their bodies, never to be divided.

—Alma 2:43-45

Jesus said unto her, I am the resurrection, and the life: he that believeth in me, though he were dead, yet shall he live: And whosoever liveth and believeth in me shall never die.

—John 11:25, 26

They must rise just as they died; we can there hail our lovely infants with the same glory— the same loveliness in the celestial glory, where they all enjoy alike. They differ in stature, in size, the same glorious spirit gives them the likeness of glory and bloom; the old man with his silvery hairs will glory in bloom and beauty. No man can describe it to you—no man can write it.

—Joseph Smith

I KNOW THAT MY REDEEMER LIVES

I know that my Redeemer lives;
What comfort this sweet sentence gives!
He lives, he lives, who once was dead.
He lives, my ever living head.
He lives to bless me with his love.
He lives to plead for me above.
He lives my hungry soul to feed.
He lives to bless in time of need.

He lives to grant me rich supply,
He lives to guide me with his eye.
He lives to comfort me when faint.
He lives to hear my soul's complaint.
He lives to silence all my fears.
He lives to wipe away my tears.
He lives to calm my troubled heart.
He lives all blessings to impart.

He lives, my kind, wise, heav'nly friend.
He lives and loves me to the end.
He lives, and while he lives, I'll sing.
He lives, my Prophet, Priest and King.
He lives and grants me daily breath.
He lives, and I shall conquer death.
He lives my mansion to prepare.
He lives to bring me safely there.

He lives, all glory to his name!
He lives, my Savior, still the same;
O sweet the joy this sentence gives:
"I know that my Redeemer lives!"
He lives, all glory to his name!
He lives, my Savior, still the same;
O sweet the joy this sentence gives:
"I know that my Redeemer lives!"

—Samuel Medley

Let not your heart be troubled: ye believe in God, believe also in me.

In my Father's house are many mansions: if it were not so, I would have told you. I go to prepare a place for you.

And if I go, and prepare a place for you, I will come again, and receive you unto myself; that where I am, there ye may be also.

—John

If Easter be not true,
Then faith must mount on broken wing;
Then love no more immortal spring;
Then hope must lose her mighty urge;
Life prove a phantom, death a dirge—
If Easter be not true.

If Easter be not true—
But it IS true, and Christ is risen!
And mortal spirit from its prison
Of sin and death with him may rise!
Worth-while the struggle, sure the prize,
Since Easter, aye, is true!

—Barstow

More painful to me are the thoughts of annihilation than death. If I have no expectation of seeing my father, mother, brothers, sisters and friends again, my heart would burst in a moment, and I should go down to my grave.

The expectation of seeing my friends in the morning of the resurrection cheers my soul and makes me bear up against the evils of life. It is like their taking a long journey, and on their return we meet them with increased joy.

—Joseph Smith

There will be no more mystery in the resurrection from the dead to life and everlasting light than there is in the birth of man into the world, when we understand the truth, as we will some day, as the Lord of glory instituted it.

—Joseph F. Smith

That which we call death is merely the slumber and rest of this mortal clay, and that only for a little season, while the spirit, the life, has gone to enjoy again the presence and society of those from whence it came, and to whom it is joy again to return. And this will be the condition of the righteous until the morning of the resurrection, when the spirit will have power to call forth the lifeless frame to be united again, and they both become a living soul, an immortal being, filled with the light and power of God. I am a witness of these things.

—Joseph F. Smith

Would you think it strange if I relate what I have seen in a vision in relation to this interesting theme? Those who have died in Jesus Christ may expect to enter into all that fruition of joy when they come forth, which they possessed or anticipated here.

So plain was the vision, that I actually saw men, before they had ascended from the tomb, as though they were getting up slowly. They took each other by the hand and said to each other, "My father, my son, my mother, my daughter, my brother, my sister." And when the voice calls for the dead to arise, suppose I am laid by the side of my father, what would be the first joy of my heart? To meet my father, my mother, my brother, my sister; and when they are by my side, I embrace them and they me.

—Joseph Smith

I think it has been taught by some that as we lay our bodies down they will so rise again in the resurrection with all the impediments and imperfections that they had here; and that if a wife does not love her husband in this state she cannot love him in the next. This is not so. Those who attain to the blessing of the first or celestial resurrection will be pure and holy, and perfect in body. Every man and woman that reaches to this unspeakable attainment will be as beautiful as the angels that surround the throne of God. If you can, by faithfulness in this life, obtain the right to come up in the morning of the resurrection, you need entertain no fears that the wife will be dissatisfied with her husband, or the husband with the wife; for those of the first resurrection will be free from sin and from the consequences and power of sin.

—Brigham Young

I have often thought that, to see a dead body, and to see that body laid in the grave and covered with earth, is one of the most gloomy things on earth; without the Gospel it is like taking a leap in the dark. But as quick as we obtain the Gospel, as soon as the spirit of man is enlightened by the inspiration of the Almighty, he can exclaim with one of old— "O grave, where is thy victory, O death, where is thy sting? The sting of death is sin, and the gift of God is eternal life, through our Lord Jesus Christ." The resurrection of the dead presents itself before the enlightened mind of man and he has a foundation for his spirit to rest upon.

—Wilford Woodruff

I f Christ lived after death, so shall men, each one taking the place in the next world for which he is best fitted. Since love is as eternal as life, the message of the resurrection is the most comforting, the most glorifying ever given to man; for when death takes a loved one from us, we can look with assurance into the open grave and say, "He is not here," and, "He will rise again."

—David O. McKay

A fter the spirit leaves the body, it remains without a tabernacle in the spirit-world until the Lord, by his law that he has ordained, brings to pass the resurrection of the dead. When the angel who holds the keys of the resurrection shall sound his trumpet, then the peculiar fundamental particles that organized our bodies here, if we do honor to them, though they be deposited in the depths of the sea, and though one particle is in the north, another in the south, another in the east, and another in the west will be brought together again in the twinkling of an eye, and our spirits will take possession of them. We shall then be prepared to dwell with the Father and the Son, and we never can be prepared to dwell with them until then. Spirits, when they leave their bodies, do not dwell with the Father and the Son, but live in the spirit world, where there are places prepared for them. Those who do honor to their tabernacles, who love and believe in the Lord Jesus Christ, must put off this mortality, or they cannot put on immortality. This body must be changed, else it cannot be prepared to dwell in the glory of the Father.

—Brigham Young

The resurrection of the body, the resurrection from the dead, is the redemption of the soul; and as Christ was the first to break the bonds of death and to take up His body, the body that had been slain, from which the spirit had temporarily departed, as by him and through him came the resurrection, by him and through him came the redemption of the soul, and hence he won for himself the title that belongs to none other, on earth or in heaven, the Redeemer of mankind.

—James E. Talmage

I shall not believe that this life is extinguished. If the Father designs to touch with divine power the cold and pulseless heart of the buried acorn, and make it to burst forth from its prison walls, will he leave neglected in the earth the soul Of man, who was made in the image of his Creator? If he stoops to give to the rosebush, whose withered blossoms float upon the breeze, the sweet assurance of another springtime, will he withhold the words of hope from the sons of men when the frosts of winter come? If matter, mute and inanimate, though changed by the forces of nature into a multitude of forms, can never die, will the imperial spirit of man suffer annihilation after it has paid a brief visit, like a royal guest, to this tenement of clay?

—William J. Bryan

There are those in the world who apparently cannot believe, or who do not believe, the information contained in the Holy Bible, that there is a resurrection for all those who die and that Jesus Christ was the first fruits of that resurrection. He came into the world, sent by his Heavenly Father to organize a church and to develop in the lives of its members an understanding of the purpose of life and to prepare them for eternal happiness, not only upon this earth in mortality, but for eternity....

I wish that all the people of the world—all our Father's children—could understand the scriptures that have been given to us by the Lord and preserved by his servants. They are replete with assurance of the resurrection and eternal life.

Of course, the outstanding evidence was that of Jesus Christ our Lord, who was crucified at Calvary, removed from the cross and laid away in the tomb. Those witnessing that great event supposed that would be the last time they would ever see him, but in three days he left the tomb, in three days his spirit had entered his immortal tabernacle and he was among his associates again.

—George Albert Smith

You will be raised from the dead just as sure as Jesus Christ was raised from the dead. As sure as by Adam you die, so sure by Christ will you be raised from the dead. This is inevitable. It is according to God's plan. He has decreed it, you cannot help yourselves. Do what you may, you cannot dodge that. It will come just as surely as birth and death come. The resurrection will come to all the children of men; but the resurrection of the righteous will come only to those who obey the commandments of the Lord.

—Joseph F. Smith

Nothing is so beautiful as a person in a resurrected and glorified condition. There is nothing more lovely than to be in this condition and have our wives and children and friends with us.

—Lorenzo Snow

After the body and spirit are separated by death, what, pertaining to this earth, shall we receive first? The body; that is the first object of a divine affection beyond the grave. We first come in possession of the body.... Some person holding the keys of the resurrection, having previously passed through that ordeal, will be delegated to resurrect our bodies, and our spirits will be there and prepared to enter into their bodies.

—Brigham Young

The Lord has told us that if we respond to certain of the gospel principles and conform to certain requirements, not only will we be resurrected with all of our children but that we shall also come forth in the morning of the first resurrection crowned with glory and eternal life, that the Church of the Firstborn shall inherit his highest and most glorious blessings and shall achieve that station in life—in the life hereafter which he has pronounced as the greatest of all exaltation in the celestial kingdom of our God.

—Stephen L Richards

Every man, woman and child will rise from the dead, will come up precisely as he [Christ] did, because there is no other name given under heaven by which we will be saved, neither is there any other way provided by which man can be raised again from death to live, but by the way instituted by the son of God.

—Joseph F. Smith

All must come forth from the grave, some time or other, in the selfsame tabernacle that they possessed while living on the earth. It will be just as Ezekiel has described it—bone will come to its bone, and flesh and sinew will cover the skeleton, and at the Lord's bidding breath will enter the body, and we shall appear, many of us, a marvel to ourselves.

—John Taylor

I believe ... that the resurrection is as well attested by credible witnesses and records as any other event in history of equal antiquity. It has often been challenged, but never disproved. Millions and millions of people have had and do now have an inner conviction of the truth of this record, and it has brought to them and continues to bring to them more comfort and more enduring hope than comes from any other source in the whole wide world. The story persists through the centuries of time because it is true. Christ lived a mortal life, died, and rose from the grave that you and I and all mankind might have everlasting life.

—Stephen L. Richards

We believe that Christ...was crucified upon the cross, that he died, his Spirit leaving his body, and was buried and was on the third day resurrected, his Spirit and body re-uniting...that he is a resurrected being, and that in his pattern every man, woman, and child that ever lived shall come forth from the grave a resurrected being, even as Christ is a resurrected being.

—Heber J. Grant

In the resurrection of the dead the child that was buried in its infancy will come up in the form of the child that it was when it was laid down; then it will begin to develop. From the day of the resurrection, the body will develop until it reaches the full measure of the stature of its spirit, whether it be male or female.

—Joseph F. Smith

The body and the spirit shall be eternally united and...there will come a time, through the blessing and mercy of God, when we will no more have sorrow, but when we shall have conquered all of these things that are of a trying and distressing character and shall stand up in the presence of the living God, filled with joy and peace and satisfaction.

—Heber J. Grant

While I was upon my knees praying, my room was filled with light. I looked up and a messenger stood by my side. I arose, and this personage told me he had come to instruct me. He presented before me a panorama. He told me he wanted me to see with my eyes and understand with my mind what was coming to pass in the earth before the coming of the Son of Man. He commenced with what the revelations say about the sun being turned to darkness, the moon to blood, and the stars falling from heaven. These things were all presented to me one after another, as they will be, I suppose, when they are manifest before the coming of the Son of Man.

Then he showed me the resurrection of the dead—what is termed the first and second resurrection. In the first resurrection I saw no graves, nor anyone raised from the grave. I saw legions of celestial beings, men and women who had received the gospel, all clothed in white robes. In the form they were presented to me, they had already been raised from the grave. After this, he showed me what is termed the second resurrection. Vast fields of graves were before me, and the Spirit of God rested upon the earth like a shower of gentle rain, and when that fell upon the graves they were opened, and an immense host of human beings came forth. They were just as diversified in their dress as we are here, or as they were laid down. This personage taught me with regard to these things.

—Wilford Woodruff

We are here in circumstances to bury our dead according to the order of the priesthood. But some of our brethren die upon the ocean; they cannot be buried in a burying ground, but they are sewed up in canvas and cast into the sea, and perhaps in two minutes after they are in the bowels of the shark, yet those persons will come forth in the resurrection, and receive all the glory of which they are worthy, and be clothed upon with all the beauty of resurrected Saints, as much so as if they had been laid away in a gold or silver coffin, and in a place expressly for burying the dead.

—Brigham Young

We will meet the same identical beings that we associated with here in the flesh—not some other soul, some other being, or the same being in some other form, but the same identity and the same form and likeness, the same person we knew and were associated with in our mortal existence, even to the wounds in the flesh. Not that a person will always be marred by scars, wounds, deformities, defects, or infirmities, for these will be removed in their course, in their proper time according to the merciful providences of God. Deformity will be removed; defects will be eliminated; and men and women shall attain to the perfection that God designed in the beginning. It is his purpose that men and women shall be made perfect, physically, as well as spiritually, through obedience to the law by which he provided the means that perfection shall come to all his children.

—Joseph F. Smith

The resurrection is just as real as death. It is also just as far reaching as death. Whether we want to or not, we die. And whether we want to or not, we shall be resurrected, all of us. There will be no exceptions. "As in Adam all die; even so in Christ shall all be made alive."

The resurrection will not change our individuality, either. We will be persons then, as now. We will recognize each other, enjoy our loved ones, and otherwise have a real, personal existence.

Death does not destroy our personality. Neither does the resurrection. Our personalities survive all things. They will survive all the changes incident to death and resurrection.

—Mark E. Petersen

The first time Jesus appeared to his disciples they thought it was a spirit that had appeared to them, and to show them that he had his tabernacle with him, he says, Bring me something to eat, and I will prove to you that there is something more than spirit in me, "What have you to eat?" And they answered, "We have got some fish here and some honey." "Bring me some fish and honey comb." And he took some of the fish and some honey and ate it before them. Now, says he, "be believing; the spirit has not flesh and bones as ye see me have."

Here was an immortal being raised from the dead. In what did that tabernacle differ from the mortal tabernacle? Was there a change wrought upon it? Had it the same eyes in its sockets, same tongue in its head, same hands and feet, with the same hole made by driving the nails through them, the same hole made in its side by the spear that was run into it? Says he, "Spirit has not flesh and bones as you see me have," and he used the same teeth, the same organs, and ate before them, and showed them that there was his tabernacle. Then wherein did he differ from the mortal tabernacle? I answer, the blood was spilled, and that the purpose of the Father might be accomplished, he caused the soldiers to run the spear into his vitals that they might draw out the last drop of his heart's blood. And when he was raised from the dead he was quickened by the spirit, by the spirit and power of the Father, and the life that was in him was not the life infused by the circulation of the blood, it was not that that kept the machinery of his organism in motion, it was the cement called spirit. And this is the essential difference between the mortal and immortal.

—Erastus Snow

Nearly two thousand years ago a man who took upon himself mortality, was crucified on the cross, his heartbeats were stilled, his loved ones grieved, and his body was silently placed in the tomb. No matter how many critics try to explain it away, those things are facts. Nineteen hundred years later, that Being appeared to the Prophet Joseph Smith, personally—not just in a dream, not in imagination, but in reality. And if one Being who took upon himself mortality, born of mortal woman, can pass through those stages, so can each one of us.

—David O. McKay

All your losses will be made up to you in the resurrection, provided you continue faithful. By the vision of the Almighty I have seen it.

—Joseph Smith

Resurrection and spring are happily associated, not that there is anything in nature exactly analogous to the resurrection, but there is so much which suggests the awakening thought. Like the stillness of death, old winter has held all vegetable life in his grasp, but as spring approaches the tender, life-giving power of heat and light compels him to relinquish his grip, and what seems to have been dead comes forth in newness of life, refreshed, invigorated, strengthened after a peaceful sleep.

So it is with man. What we call death, Jesus referred to as sleep. "Lazarus sleepeth," he said to his disciples. "The damsel sleepeth," were his comforting words to the bereaved and sorrowing parents of a little girl. Indeed, to the Savior of the world there is no such thing as death—only life—eternal life. Truly he could say, "I am the resurrection, and the life: he that believeth in me, though he were dead, yet shall he live." (John 11:25.)

—David O. McKay

And when he had spoken these things, while they beheld, he was taken up; and a cloud received him out of their sight.

And, while they looked stedfastly toward heaven as he went up, behold, two men stood by them in white apparel;

Which also said, Ye men of Galilee, why stand ye gazing up into heaven? this same Jesus, which is taken up from you into heaven, shall so come in like manner as ye have seen him go into heaven.

—Acts 1:9-11

The veil was taken from our minds, and the eyes of our understanding were opened.

We saw the Lord standing upon the breastwork of the pulpit, before us; and under his feet was a paved work of pure gold, in color like amber.

His eyes were as a flame of fire; the hair of his head was white like the pure snow; his countenance shone above the brightness of the sun; and his voice was as the sound of the rushing of great waters, even the voice of Jehovah, saying:

I am the first and the last; I am he who liveth, I am he who was slain; I am your advocate with the Father.

—D&C 110:1-4

And now, after the many testimonies which have been given of him, this is the testimony, last of all, which we give of him: That he lives!

For we saw him, even on the right hand of God; and we heard the voice bearing record that he is the Only Begotten of the Father—

That by him, and through him, and of him, the worlds are and were created, and the inhabitants thereof are begotten sons and daughters unto God.

—Ibid., 76:22-24